Contents

Pass It On

Pass It On

Karen A. Livingston

iUniverse, Inc.
New York Lincoln Shanghai

Pass It On

iUniverse, Inc.

For information address:
iUniverse, Inc.
2021 Pine Lake Road, Suite 100
Lincoln, NE 68512
www.iuniverse.com

ISBN: 0-595-32501-7 (pbk)
ISBN: 0-595-66610-8 (cloth)

Printed in the United States of America

To my family, who has put up with the antics that seem to follow me; the "boys", who are usually the source of the antics; and the "Friday Night Crew" and Rose, who helped show me the wonder of those antics.

Preface

Why write this book? I have often asked myself this same question, and the only answer I can come up with is my desire to assist those who are in the same predicament that I found myself in over 20 years ago. Back then, the field of metaphysics was left to those who were believed to be "chemically imbalanced" and therefore lacking in their capacity to reason and function in the "real world." The only options left to those of us who were apparently sane and truly interested in this field were secret visits to self-proclaimed psychics or fortunetellers, or behind-door classes offered through word of mouth.

However, as time passes by and more of us are willing to discuss this once taboo topic, I find myself repeatedly reciting the events that have brought me to where I am today. Those occurrences that have in some way confirmed that those chemically challenged people may not have been as eccentric as they were once thought to be.

Everything in this book is based upon my own beliefs and experiences. I originally set out to create a sort of handbook to be given to anyone who would ask me about my feelings on the topic of metaphysics or parapsychology. My aim was to take several aspects and touch upon each one briefly, thereby creating a guide for someone who was just starting out. I do not claim to be an expert in any of the topics discussed. I only wish to offer the reader my opinions so that they may have a glimpse into our world and, hopefully, so that they too will choose to join the rest of us who find themselves the "lost souls" among the living.

Introduction

I was born in the "Age of Aquarius." A time when people theorized that all that the world needed to heal itself was love sweet love. While growing up I believed, as I still do, in the concept that we are not alone. That unseen forces, whether we choose to call them angels or spirit guides, do exist, and help to guide us on the path that has been chosen for us—the path called life. I follow the ideals of reincarnation and karma. The fundamental principle that we are not put here for one lifetime to prove ourselves worthy of the ultimate eternal happiness we have all been taught about in one way or another. It is my belief that God gives us many chances to redeem our souls and learn the lessons that are needed to achieve "Heaven." That eventually everyone acquires the wisdom that is necessary for the privilege of being a soul at peace with God.

In this book I hope to recount the events that have helped to confirm those beliefs. Those experiences which occur in our day-to-day lives, not during some hypnotic trance, séance, or psychic consultation. To relay to the reader my philosophy that there are not only extraordinary people in this world who possess these unique talents of communication, but to submit to you the theory that these talents to connect with the unseen realm lie within all of us. That all we need to do is to learn how to master them. Believe me, I was just as frustrated as the next person when I began; and it is my hope that, by passing on my experiences to others, they may able to utilize this knowledge and gain some insight as to what is out there.

So where does a person begin, you may ask. One can become totally confused when confronting ideas of karma, auras, chakras, and channeling. In this book I will do my best to help the reader "start from the beginning," the basics. I offer suggestions obtained through my own experiences, and those of others whom I have encountered along the way. Whether acquired through a seminar, readings, or just sitting around in a meditation group talking, these suggestions have helped me and many others in our search for answers in the metaphysical realm.

When I speak of my friends and meditation group throughout this book, I want you to know that this group consists of office workers, nurses, housewives, teachers, computer technicians, laborers, etc. They are both male and female. To put it more simply, they are ordinary people. The one common bond we all share is curiosity and the belief that we are not alone. None of us took specialized courses that made us master psychics or mediums. The learning occurs as we go along.

How is it, though, that this knowledge was acquired? Yes, some workshops were attended, and some have read numerous books on the subject. However, most of us have just sat and listened to stories of the personal accounts of others. And, just as it was before the invention of the written word, we draw on the knowledge or lessons gained by our listening, and then utilize the information to improve on our own lives. Thus, I have chosen to write down what understanding I have attained in a narrative format.

Certainly most of us have learned something from the experiences of others, in addition to gaining what knowledge we must from our own experiences. For, if we really look closely at it, what is life but the soul on a journey to gain wisdom? And once we have obtained that wisdom, hopefully, we pass it on...

PART I

Faith is...

>...the knowledge that at the end of the tunnel, there will be light.

>...the realization that through the journey of life, we do not walk alone.

>...the acceptance of advice from one who has been there.

>...the courage to let go.

>...the strength to go on.

SECTION 1
FAITH

Your faith is the one thing that nobody can take away from you. They can take your possessions, they can take your freedom, they can even take your life; but they can never take away your faith. This has been evident all throughout history. During most periods of religious persecution or slavery, the one common strength possessed by all who were oppressed was their strong faith. Whether it was the Christians, Jews, or Africans, to mention a few, when times were hardest, one need not look far to see or hear these individuals singing their praises to God. To look at the inhumane treatment endured by these societies, one would think that they would lose their faith in a God that would allow such treatment to persist. However, this was not the case. In fact, the exact opposite seemed true; the harder the times, the stronger their faith became.

The reason for my beginning with this topic is that one should not even think about venturing into the realm of the metaphysical without a strong belief in someone or something out there protecting you. It does not matter where the foundation lies, only that it exists. I have found that the majority of people will seek out help from the "other side" when times get hardest, or when they are confronted with something that they wish to resolve right away. I have learned, along with quite a few others, that this is not an area to "dabble in" or to seek out quick relief. You may find that instead of helping, it might just jump up and scare the hell out of you. Then you will find yourself with the same problems or dilemmas, in addition to sleeping at night with the lights on staring at the ceiling and a Bible clenched in your hands.

Therefore, if you have faith, strengthen it. If you have lost your faith, find it; and if you do not have faith, acquire it.

As for my own beliefs, I have found that just by looking for the few common factors which underlie all religious beliefs, and following them, one really cannot go wrong. To put it more simply, all your bases will be covered. I am very proud of this ideology, especially since I found out recently, while reading a biography on Benjamin Franklin, that he followed the same premise when it came to religion. (I guess great minds think alike.) During my lifetime there have been many times when I could have given up and fallen into the learned helplessness syndrome. However, as history has shown, it was at these times that I turned to my faith in God. Believe me, most times it can become quite a tug of war when I should just hand my troubles over and let Him handle them, but eventually I realize that I cannot change anything with worry, and so I let go.

So please remember, whenever you decide to take a peek into that mystifying world of the unknown, do not forget to bring your faith along for the ride. You never know when it might just come in handy.

During a meditation on Good Friday in 1996, I received a story pertaining to the subject of faith that I decided to present at this point in my book to reinforce my position on the topic.

A MESSAGE FROM ABOVE

There once was a grumpy old man who lived outside a village. Nobody would bother with him, for whenever they tried to talk to him, he would spew words of pessimism and doom. He would complain that life was a miserable thing and there was really nothing to look forward to. However, to the amazement of all the villagers, he was able to grow the most magnificent garden and sell the flowers. If it were not for this wonderful skill, no one would bother with him at all.

One day a woman named Kaye went to buy some flowers for a sick friend and, being at a loss for a topic of conversation, started to speak with the old man about religion. "Oh, don't start spewing that nonsense about some wondrous God who lived, suffered, and died and then rose from the dead at me!" he complained. "That garbage is for fools, of which one I am not. There is only one thing in this world that one can depend on, and that is flowers! Now take your purchase and please go" he raved. With that Kaye left the garden not knowing why she had bothered in the first place.

A few months later, not knowing why, Kaye decided to return to the garden thinking that maybe there was some way that she could get through to this unhappy old soul. Maybe she could convince him that all was not as dismal as he made it. Kaye ventured precariously up the walk, and to her surprise, was greeted not by the old man's usual scowl, but with a splendid glowing smile. Kaye proceeded very carefully fearing that at any moment the man's usual grumpy demeanor would return. She approached slowly and inquired, "I noticed that your mood seems a bit different today. If you do not mind me asking, has something happened?" He looked at me with eyes that glowed with a strange sparkle and responded, "Have a seat and allow me to explain."

Kaye went over and sat down in the chair he was indicating and listened intently as he spoke.

> *"One day while I was tending my garden a young man came in to purchase flowers. When I looked up at him I found that he had the most beautiful eyes I had ever seen. He started a conversation and no matter how hard I tried to avoid responding to him, he just kept talking and asking questions about my gardening. "Why is this, and how is that....?" He just kept at me until I could no longer avoid him. Then he asked me the one question that would change my life. "How is it," he inquired holding up a beautiful Lily "that such a magnificent flower could bloom to bring such happiness to those who look upon it, then die only to return again another day to spread that happiness once more?" "What are you talking about?" I snapped back. "Why are you asking me such a stupid question? How would I know the answer to that question? I just have confidence that nature knows what it is doing, that the Lily will be reborn and it is!" "But what about conditions that could damage it during the time it lays dormant, such as cold or drought? How do you know it will make it through?" The young man questioned further. "Because I have faith in nature and know that it will take care of its own!" I ranted back. The young man just smiled back at me and said "That is a wonderful answer. It gives one a sense of peace believing in something which does not let you down, doesn't it?" Suddenly he was circled with a glorious light and looked at me with such love in his eyes as he asked, "Now if you can accept that of such a simple thing as a flower in nature, how can you doubt it of me and my promise to you?" With that he touched my head and smiled. "Now continue spreading the beauty of nature throughout the world, but from now on spread my messages along with it." And with those words he was gone.*

Kaye stood and listened in amazement about the miracle that had transformed this cynical old man into a happy soul filled with faith. When the old man was done telling his story, he once again smiled and returned to his garden. For the first time, Kaye left that garden with a warm sense of peace and contentment, for her own faith had also been strengthened by the old man's revelation.

I have taken a path which I chose to travel

The mysteries of the world I had hoped to unravel

Sometimes there were smiles; at times there were tears

So much has happened over so many years

And the stories of my journey I here now impart

But where to begin...

Why not at the start?

SECTION 2
IN THE BEGINNING...

I was in my teens when I was actually introduced to the field of metaphysics. My mother brought me to a woman who, I feel, had acquired the wisdom of the ages. For lack of a better term I will use the phrase "psychic." This woman exhibited such understanding and insight that one could not help but be astounded by her abilities. To use the old joke, not only could she tell you what color underwear you had on, she could also tell you what size they were, and when they were last washed. She was, and still is, the oldest soul I have ever known. I would sit and watch in amazement as she answered other people's questions during her group sessions (for which she charged a whopping three dollars); only to learn later from these same individuals that she was correct 99% of the time. Needless to say, after meeting her, my eagerness to learn all that I could about this mystical realm increased with each opportunity that arose.

At one point I decided to take a course on psychic awareness. This was not a simple task to accomplish. Believe me, finding a place that offered classes in the paranormal was not an easy task in the early 1980's. I did, however, manage to find one in Yonkers, New York, and set out one night every week with a notebook in hand and an open mind.

During one such class the instructor explained that headaches may not just be a physical ailment, they might be a force or energy from the other side trying to get in contact with you for some reason or another. In the course of the week following that class, a strange incident occurred which I could not find any explanation for. In the days following the event I developed one of the most severe headaches I had ever had. It stayed with me through to the next class, where I eventually found myself having trouble concentrating.

Unexpectedly one of my classmates, whom I will refer to as Jan, looked over at me and said, "He is here for you," pointing into the darkened room next to me. Now taking into consideration that I was new to this stuff, and that *The Exorcist* was the movie of the times, I just looked at her and told her that she must be mistaken. "No," she explained, "He has come for you." All of a sudden the room disappeared and I felt as if I were viewing a movie of an open field on a large screen. The scene played out (an actual account of the events are detailed in Section 8 of this book) and it seemed as if Jan and I were the only ones in the room witnessing what was taking place. Without getting into all the details now, the outcome was that I had been sent back to view a past life, which incidentally explained the strange incident that had occurred the week before. The "person" who had come for me wound up being the first guide that would work with me in my pursuit of the mysteries of the spirit world, my "Doc."

However, the night was not to end there. After the surroundings calmed and everything became clear, the room suddenly became very cold. I looked over at Jan and she was shaking. She looked at me with a panic evident in her eyes and said that she did not want to deal with the other "entity" which had shown up and was pushing its way in. I looked over toward the instructor, only to find the same look of panic in his eyes, and realized that no one else was offering to help this woman. The next few minutes became what I will call an "out of body" experience. My faith seemed to take over where my sensibility left off. My mind screamed for me to get out of the house as I "watched" myself walk over to Jan, remove my protective talisman from my neck, and hand it to her. As my mind continued ranting at me that I was crazy for doing it, I watched with amazement as I proceeded to take Jan's hand and recite the entire *Footprints* prayer to her. I should mention that I never knew the prayer word for word, but for some strange reason I was able to recall it in its entirety that night. I explained to Jan that she was not alone, that she was protected and did not have to deal with any energy that she felt uncomfortable about. That all she needed to do was to ask it to leave.

Ultimately, the room began to warm up and everything seemed to calm down. I eventually felt myself return to my body. Anger overtook me as I confronted the instructor on his inability to deal with the situation. I felt, and feel still, that anyone who claims the knowledge of a subject enough to teach others should be able to handle any problem that may arise, especially when dealing with the realm of the supernatural.

Needless to say, I never returned to class; however to this day my friendship with Jan still remains one of my most treasured. We both came away from class that evening with a message which will remain with us forever; the assurance that we are not alone. It has been over twenty years now, and we continue to work together seeking out the "wisdom of the universe." I must say though that whenever I look back on that night I find myself thanking God that I did not leave my faith at home that evening.

When all the world is full of stress,

And life seems such an awful mess,

Shut off the lights, slow down the pace,

And find yourself a quiet place.

SECTION 3
MEDITATION

Meditation plays one of the most important roles in parapsychology, yet most individuals are under the assumption that it is a difficult thing to do. On the contrary, if we allow ourselves to really sit back and relax, the process is not hard at all. It is when we release the stress and give ourselves over to the meditative state that we are truly able to connect with the "other side" and receive the answers we seek.

Meditation can be done alone or with others. I have found that a group environment yields the best results at first, which my astrologer sister has advised me is a typical way of thinking for an Aquarius. I notice that a group setting offers one the opportunity to relate their expectations, doubts, or fears openly. In addition, the suggestions and shared experiences of others may help an individual along in their progression. A little bit of advice: try to refrain from the use of alcohol or drugs while meditating. They serve no purpose here.

The first step in the process of meditation is to find a quiet place, where there will be as little distraction as possible from the outside world. I agree with the notion that every home has a "heart," a section where the energy is the most conducive for any sort of metaphysical activity. Locating this spot is not as difficult as it may seem. Sometimes we find it totally by accident. It usually is the place where you will find your favorite chair, or where you are most comfortable reading, or working on your hobbies. If you find that you are having a problem locating the area, there are those who can assist you. But please, do not let them charge you $200.00 to do so! If all else fails, bring a small child into your home and ask them to help you find a special place to "play."

Once you have accomplished this task, section this area off, if you can. It is not necessary to actually build walls; I have had success in using movable walls, such as dividers, bi-fold doors, or changing screens. Paint or decorate the walls with colors or patterns favorable for relaxation, and encircle yourself with calming, peaceful objects. I find using plenty of candlelight and surrounding myself with relaxation music to be extremely beneficial.

You are now ready to begin the new experience of meditation. Think of everything people have told you about meditation, all the things you have read, all the movies you have seen, then FORGET them! Meditation is what you make of it. It does not necessarily have to come in any shape or form. There is no "right way" to meditate. The most important thing is that you are comfortable doing it, in whichever way that is. Some people perform little rituals to get them into the meditative state, while others just sit quietly and pray. I know of someone who would fall asleep every time she meditated, so one night she told us that she was going to stand up during our session.

During meditation I have discovered that the messages come in various ways. Some people hear things, while others see. Some just "sense" energies, while others smell aromas. At first many people don't get anything, and this may become frustrating, but please do not give up. Try to refrain from putting pressure on yourself to miraculously gain all the knowledge of the universe at once, it takes time. Just continue meditating, if only for its relaxation benefits, and eventually you will open up enough to begin receiving information. And please try your best not to be afraid; it only serves to close you down. That is why I recommend the group setting at first, with someone who is a little more advanced in the subject. Someone you trust enough to let yourself go and know that they will be there to offer help if you find you need it.

To put the group at ease, I also suggest a protection meditation at the beginning of each session, and a cleansing meditation upon completion. Basic meditations can be found in books, on the Internet, or improvised. Taped guided meditations also offer assistance to those who are having trouble starting.

The one thing that you must take into meditation is your imagination. Contrary to popular belief, you actually use it to begin each session. "Imagine yourself on a beach, on a mountain, in a forest...," are the beginning of many guided meditations. As you progress you will find that you can tell the difference between what is "imagined" and what is real. As you grow more at ease with the meditation process, you can request validations as a means of helping you confirm that information is being drawn from another source, and not your own imagination. Most importantly, never believe that anything coming through is "too silly" or cannot possibly mean anything. I have found the most ridiculous things to be validations for the person I am helping. **Do not edit**. Say whatever comes through, for it is meant to be understood the way it is presented.

Meditation can benefit us in so many ways. Whether by delving within our own subconscious mind for answers, seeking answers from beyond, assisting us in prayer, or just lowering our blood pressure. So sit back, relax, and enjoy the experience.

I learned a lesson well taught today

The teacher had great things to say

This teacher has taught me many times before

But no matter how often, I'll always seek more

And I'll not complain as each lesson is piled

For I love this teacher...he is my child.

SECTION 4
THE CHILD BECOMES
THE TEACHER

Have you ever watched a child at play with the entity labeled by the "sane" world as their imaginary friend? They can go on for hours chatting away with what most people believe to be thin air. And that enjoyable tea party, which we never seem to have time to join them in, can continue on without us. We have heard numerous tales of children being able to see people who have passed on, and been questioned by our little ones about the person in the picture who has died but is now standing over by the window.

As I have mentioned earlier, I believe that we all possess the capabilities that would enable us to tap into the "other side." We are born into this world each lifetime with a little more knowledge buried in our subconscious mind than before. As we pass from lifetime to lifetime, we find it easier to reach into our inner self and utilize those talents. As a child we do not know that we are not supposed to exhibit the ability to see or hear someone who is not physically there. We sense the energy, hear the whispers and, until we are told otherwise, enjoy the time they spend with us. It is the adult world which tells us that everything is our imagination, and that as we grow older we should put aside those childish beliefs. They advise us that we should only believe in what we can see and touch. Yet, they also tell us that we should believe in a God and his associates, whether we choose to call them saints or angels, whom we are not able to see or touch. No wonder most children go through periods of frustration, wouldn't you?

A long time ago I decided to raise my children with my beliefs. Oh, trust me; I had much resistance from my spouse, who was raised in the Roman Catholic faith. We eventually came to a compromise and life at home got a little easier. Let's face it, both ideals are based in the Christian faith and the foundation is the same. Eventually all end up in paradise, it is just the path we choose to get there on, and how long it actually takes to arrive, that differs.

There were several periods in my children's lives when they exhibited the abilities I have mentioned, whether it was my daughter questioning who the new "person" in the kitchen was, or my son hearing voices calling his name. I would never offer contradiction, only confirmation. I would sit down with each one and try to explain what each occurrence meant for them at that point in their life. I would let them know how wonderful it was that there would always be someone there for them, keeping them company and watching over them, especially when I was not around to do so.

SPOOKED

One evening while away on vacation my husband Robert and I were sharing a bedroom with my two children. Since my husband had perfected the art of snoring, I was not able to sleep so I opted for the couch in the living room. At approximately 2:30 am Robert jumped onto the couch shivering. When I asked him what was wrong he told me the following story.

It seems that he had woken up from his sleep to find our son Robbie standing by the bedroom door looking at him. When my husband asked my son what was wrong, Robbie wouldn't answer him. Again Robert questioned, "Robbie why are you standing there? Are you looking for Mommy?" and again my son just stood there and stared. Annoyed, Robert arose from his bed to switch on the bedroom light. When he turned to look at my son, he could not find him. He turned towards the bed and found Robbie sound asleep next to his sister. What frightened Robert was the fact that Robbie could not have returned to the bed without passing his father.

I guess Robbie had chosen that evening to demonstrate to his father his skill of astrotraveling.

NEW KID IN TOWN

Our guides come and go all through our lives. During a meditation session one early May evening a new guide decided to make a "grand" entrance into my life. As we all sat around relaxed in our meditative state, this one energy glided into the room demanding attention, and when he was displeased with the amount he was receiving, he decided to make a nuisance of himself. After I explained to our new "friend" that he would have to leave if he was not able to cooperate, he sulked off and quietly watched over the group from the corner of the room. When the session ended we all had a good laugh about the situation and everyone left. I went off to bed forgetting about our new guest for the evening.

While at work the next day I received a call from my daughter. She had just arrived home from school and wanted to know who the big grumpy guy standing in the corner of the living room was.

While we are on the subject of teachers…

SECTION 5
FINDING THE RIGHT TEACHER

While completing an essay for her college application my daughter wrote the following lines, "I consider my teachers to be my inspiration in life. They are the heroes for me because without them we would not have the people society labels as heroes. We would not have doctors, scientists, astronauts, or others that people look up to today." These lines make more sense than she may have realized. For without teachers, where would we be? In the Christian religion, Christ himself chose to come into this world in the form of a teacher. In fact, if we examine most religions, the main deity takes on the role of teacher.

As I mentioned in a previous chapter, my first "teacher" in the subject of parapsychology was a disappointment. Considering the situation, it is my opinion that he was not qualified or experienced enough to handle the situation that arose. Since the field of parapsychology is very ambiguous, it is probably fair to say that it would be difficult to research a formidable teacher on the subject. However, one should be comfortable with the one they choose. You should ask questions until you are satisfied that the individual can offer you the knowledge and opportunity to advance your talents. I am of the opinion that the amount of experience, not degrees, a person possesses is of utmost importance. Through the years I have been confronted with several individuals who have claimed to be experts on the subject. Some were, and some were lacking. A teacher should be one who is also willing to be taught something new everyday. They should not claim to be the "all knowing" and place aside the thoughts of his or her student. In the metaphysical field there are many areas which are still uncharted, and who knows when the next "great guru" will come along, or what form they will take? Another type of parapsychologist I choose to stay away from is one who claims that they have a "special gift." We all possess the ability to utilize these talents, it is just where we happen to be in the process of learning that determines the extent to which we are able to use them.

So keep seeking out the one person who you feel will help you to achieve the next level in this journey we call life. As in most fields, it is not necessarily the most expensive; after all Christ did it for free.

I came across my guide today,

And this is what he had to say.

"I'll be with you each day you breathe,

To call upon whenever you need.

You cannot reach me with a phone,

But always know, you are not alone.

For I have been chosen to lend you a hand

To show you the way, whatever is planned.

Each smile you smile, I smile with you,

Each tear you cry, I'll help you through.

No matter what path in life you choose,

I'm here to guide you, win or lose."

This affirmation he gave to me,

Left me with such serenity.

And I can be content to say,

I came across my guide today.

SECTION 6
GUIDES

"I want to meet my guide. Do you see anyone with me?, How come I can't see anything?, Could you ask my guide…." These are just a few of the questions I am asked when I relay the method of how I meet and work with my guides. I have thought long and hard about how to respond to these individuals. What could I tell them to do that would bring them face to face with the most cherished individual from the "other side?"

I have come to the realization that in my circle there is no special trick or meditation which will suddenly make your guide appear to you. I have even utilized hypnosis to help some people find their guides, with little success. Oh, I took the required courses and performed the right steps, but they just didn't appear. Don't get me wrong, I am not saying that you're guide will not appear to you under these circumstances, they might. What I'm saying is that it just does not seem to work for me that way. For me, when the time comes for a person to start actually working together with their guides, they seem to just "pop in." Some people have what I would call hidden guides who never really "show" themselves, they just guide. Others, like myself, seem to draw the more flamboyant guides who do not just pop in; they make a grand entrance like in some scene from a movie. Now while this may sound wonderful to you, believe me, at times it can be very unnerving. I have found, however, that there is a third type of guide that likes an "introduction." In other words, when the time is right, they seek out a friend of the individual who is, shall we say, "tuned in" and create their own "How do you do?" session.

To better illustrate this point, the following sections give some occasions on which this has happened.

LADY IN GREEN

I have been told many times that I draw my best energy from mountainous terrains. This comes as no surprise to me, for most of our family vacations have been spent hiking in every wooded area on the eastern seaboard. Each family member knows that if you vacation with the Livingstons you must commit to one day of trekking through the woods appreciating nature, whether you like it or not.

In the summer of 2000 a busy schedule had not allowed for the usual vacation in the woods. One day in July I had decided that my energy level was a little low, a deficiency that I had also been feeling during my meditations. My niece was visiting from Florida and one evening, as we sat at the dinner table, I announced to the family that we would find the closest mountain possible and spend a day hiking. After the moaning stopped, and my husband announced that he "unfortunately" had to work, I told them that we would leave for Bear Mountain early the next morning.

As the sun rose on a beautiful summer morning, despite my fourteen-year-old daughter Amanda's prayers for rain, I dragged everyone out of bed and she, my ten-year-old son Robbie, my niece, and I began our adventure. Forty five minutes later we stood staring at a billboard of the Bear Mountain hiking trails. "Which trail are we taking?" my son eagerly asked. "Hopefully the shortest one" was his sister's reply. "Hey, this is my vacation, what are you grumbling about?" came my niece's response, and I knew I was in for a "wonderful" excursion.

Up we climbed, with Robbie in the lead and Amanda pulling up the rear, complaining all the way. Halfway into the trail, I decided to give the kids a break and let them sit a while. After taking some pictures and placing a call to sing *The Sound of Music* over the telephone to our friend, we all sat quietly staring out at the beautiful landscape, or at least I did; the kids threw things at each other. As the wind blew and the smell of pine permeated my nasal cavity, I looked over at my niece and saw a woman in a green flowing dress standing by her. Since my niece was only eighteen at the time, and had heard several stories about her crazy Aunt Karen, I decided to tread lightly. "Do you know what a guide is?" I inquired, to which she said yes. "Do you know that you have a lady in green as one of your guides?" I advised. "How do you know?" she asked. "Well, she is standing right beside you and for some reason she wants me to mention the tulips in your bedroom," I responded. At this statement everyone looked strangely at me, for they all knew that my niece was your typical tomboy. Her bedroom consisted of baseball paraphernalia, softball trophies, and everything far from a flowery little girl's room. "It doesn't make sense to me either," I confessed, "but this is what she is showing me as a validation that she belongs to you." "Sorry to disappoint you Aunt Karen, but there are no tulips, or anything with flowers, in my bedroom," she said, and we left it at that.

Upon returning home later that evening my sister, called to check on her daughter. After relaying the information of how we dragged her into the woods for a hike, my niece recounted the story of the lady in green to her mother. After she had flippantly told my sister about the tulip, she suddenly became quiet. "Are you kidding?" my niece exclaimed after a minute or two. You see my niece had been attending a college away from home that semester and had failed to notice, prior to coming to New York, that her mother had placed a new bedspread upon her bed which had, of all things, tulips! I guess my niece's guide, the lady in green, found it as funny as we did.

MUNCHKIN LAND

One evening late in December 1995 during a meditation group session, I saw the image of a man I referred to as "Mike Brady in his hippie stage." He had curly brown hair, a tunic style shirt and a peace sign hanging around his neck. When I asked why he had appeared, he informed me that his name was Sam and that he had come to watch over his "munchkin." When the meditation session was over and everyone was asked what he or she had experienced, I mentioned Sam, and questioned if anyone had been nicknamed munchkin, or knew of anyone called by that name. Nobody could recall being labeled that or anyone connected to them being called that so I just left it alone.

That January my husband Robert was planning on visiting his parents in Florida. At the time my daughter Amanda was ten years old and had never been separated from her father for more than one day. My daughter is a typical "Daddy's little girl" and, needless to say, the prospect of him leaving was extremely unpleasant. At this point I should mention the fact that our family is into the Arts and Amanda had been performing in plays since she was seven. A nearby community theater was holding auditions for parts in their upcoming play so, to alleviate her worry over her father's leaving, I told Amanda that I would take her for an audition. Since these auditions were being held during the same week he would be away, I felt it would help to distract her.

Well, the time for Robert's departure came and, as expected, there were many tears at the airport. By mid-week we were off to auditions. After giving her resume and her best rendition of "Happy Birthday," Amanda was told that she would hear from the theater group by the end of the week. The phone rang on Friday evening and it was for Amanda. As I watched her face for the response, she quietly thanked them and hung up. "Well?" I anxiously asked. "I got a part!" she responded and started to jump up and down. Oh, by the way, did I happen to mention that the play they were putting on was *The Wiz* and that Amanda had gotten the part as one of the munchkins? Apparently, Sam was going to watch over Amanda in her father's absence.

PEARLS OF WISDOM

I have a friend I will affectionately refer to as Doubting Thomas. Don't get me wrong, he believed in everything we would discuss; he just does not believe in his own capabilities. He longed for some sort of confirmation of the fact that he was not alone, that someone or something traveled with him in this journey called life. When we would hold a meditation group, after the session was over and we would ask what each individual had experienced, he would usually start out by saying, "Well, I didn't really get anything." Sometimes I could read the frustration in his eyes even though he would never admit to it.

One evening, during a telephone conversation, he brought up the topic of his guitar lessons. As he spoke I saw the image of a woman who I described to him as looking like "Donna Reed." I told him that she was one of his guides and that she had enjoyed his playing. I was so happy because finally something had come through for him. The voice which came back to me over the telephone held the usual "that's nice" tone with its hint of doubt. I continued by telling him that she had been letting him know she was there through the lights in his apartment. "Are you kidding?" was his response. "My lights have been flickering and acting funny for the past few months." I also advised him that she was smiling and wanted me to ask him about the "shoes." To this statement he became silent. Then he explained that whenever he practiced he would put on this old pair of sneakers. He claimed that it had become so obvious that his children had begun to tease him by saying "Oh, Dad, you're going to practice, don't forget to put on the shoes."

Through these validations, it became clear that his guide's presence had been confirmed. I told him that she was showing me a pair of pearls so, therefore, he should call her Pearl. He agreed, which made me very happy because my Doubting Thomas had begun to believe.

PENNIES FROM HEAVEN

A young woman, whom I will call Mary Ellen, came to me through a friend of my husband. It seems that she had become interested in the parapsychology field and had heard about my experiences. She called and I agreed to meet with her and advise her of what I had learned thus far.

We met early one evening and wound up talking for several hours about our lives. During our meeting her guide decided to join in our group. He wanted to introduce himself and said that she would know when he was around by the pennies he left around. He brought up the date 1941, and even mentioned that there was one under her bed at this very moment. Mary Ellen could not connect anything to the 1941 date and explained that there was nothing under her bed; she was sure of this because she always checked for monsters there. She did mention though that the volume on the stereo in her room would constantly go up and down.

The next day Mary Ellen called me and said that she had found a penny under her bed when she had gotten home that evening. When I asked the date, she said it was 1979. After that night, and right through to this writing, she continues to find pennies all over the place.

The final piece to the puzzle came about six weeks later when we were chatting on the telephone. Mary Ellen was complaining that the stereo was acting up again. I had to put her on hold for a moment and when I came back on the line she was mumbling something to herself. When I asked what she was talking about she said that she had found a penny in the volume control of her stereo, and the date on it was 1941. The realization hit about two seconds later.

Please tell me my future, oh mighty soothsayer.

Will I dance the ballet or be a ball player?

Will it hold much happiness; have I lived in the past?

Will I find true love, and how long will it last?

Will I have enough money to get all that I crave?

Will I live very long, or be early to grave?

Please answer my questions of what's yet to be.

Look into my future,......what is it you see?

SECTION 7
PSYCHICS, MEDIUMS,
CLAIRVOYANTS...OH MY!

Psychic.... what a wonderful word. To truly have the ability to know what our future holds, and what path we are meant to take in this life-time. To have all the answers for those who are willing to pay enough.

As you may have assumed by now, I have a problem with the topic of "messages for money." Yes, I will agree that if someone has a gift they should be able to request some compensation for their time and effort. However, they should also keep in mind that is just what it is, a gift bestowed upon them by God. That He has chosen to use them as His messenger, and that the gift can be taken away as quickly as it was given.

There are many psychics, mediums, clairvoyants, or whatever you choose to call them, available to the public today. It is not like the days of yesteryear where you had to take a trip to a boardwalk, or sneak into back doors, to find one. Over the years I have visited quite a few myself, from mountain men to evangelic ministers. It has been my experience that most are not all they claim to be, but there are some that actually are worth the trip. You should not judge who is the best by the amount of money they charge. The best one I ever knew charged only $25 for a one on one session, and she did not even use a timer.

The individuals who really frustrate me are those who make you "guarantee" a certain number of people before they will honor you with their presence. If there are two, or ten, people present it should make no difference; whoever shows up is meant to be there, and those who do not, aren't. Another bit of advice I offer is that if someone tells you that you have an "evil spell or spirit" around you, and for $100 they can remove it, run! It is this kind of underhanded action that has given the true psychic a bad reputation.

Well, now that I have vented, let me give you some suggestions. I find that having a trusted friend sitting in on the session, when possible, can do wonders when dealing with "psychic amnesia." This is a phenomenon which sometimes occurs when we go to these individuals; many a time I have asked people questions, to which they adamantly answer "no", only to have their friend sitting beside them shaking their head "yes." If bringing a companion is not feasible, ask if you can tape the session, I have also received quite a few calls when the person leaves stating that they had incorrectly answered me. Either way, when you leave, reflect on what you have been told; messages are not always what they first seem to be. Symbolism runs rampant when dealing with communications from the other side.

In addition, remember that when you visit a psychic, take what you are told as what *might be*. Very rarely have I found anyone that has told me exactly what was going to happen, and it actually did. Do not let it discourage you though; freewill still exists and can veer you off your path at any time (I can hear the nay sayers now screaming "copout"). Keep in mind that every bump in the road happens for a reason, be patient. Furthermore, try not to waste your money by going too often; allow enough time between visits for things to come to pass (I recommend at least six months). I also do not recommend bringing children in for "readings"; childhood holds enough challenges for them without getting them mixed up with the future. Besides, as I have discussed earlier, the child could probably tell the psychic more about the nonphysical realm than the psychic could tell the child.

I looked back over my past today

The lessons learned along the way

The hurt, the pain, a love, a smile

I thought about each one a while

I acknowledged them all, both bitter and sweet

For these lessons have made my soul complete.

SECTION 8
LEARN FROM THE PAST

I am a supporter of the belief that we are not just put here on this earth for one lifetime, and that it is during that lifetime we are expected to prove ourselves worthy of "Heaven." It is my conviction, similar to that of many others, that we go through several lifetimes. Haven't we all had the experience of déjà vu where we can describe a place, never having actually been there before? Or when we are passionately lured to specific periods in history, whether through books or movies?

I believe that each lifetime is a lesson within itself, and, as lessons sometimes tend to be, some are difficult. This is why one may so often hear the phrase "this is hell." As we complete each lifetime our soul draws nearer to completion, and it is through the knowledge gained along the way that we ultimately attain paradise. Each lifetime provides us with something to add onto our list of accomplishments, or as I prefer to view it, as something more to place into our "chest of knowledge."

However, sometimes we fail to complete these lessons in the lifetime in which they occur and, ultimately, we find that those unsettled issues leave us with unresolved karma. This karma tends to surface in another lifetime and may cause us difficulties in that lifetime for no apparent reason. We may find ourselves chasing after unattainable dreams, sabotaging relationships, or even in constant states of depression, for no understandable reasons. We spend years in psychotherapy searching for answers that never come. I have even seen these unfinished matters manifest themselves as actual physical ailments. It is at these points in our lives that past life regression becomes necessary.

I was always fascinated with the past life regression experience, having gone through several myself (the first of which is described in the following pages). The amount of knowledge revealed was amazing, and they had a tendency to answer many issues influencing my current life. I even attended seminars for hypnotherapy in order to delve into the subconscious mind for answers. In time, I even became certified as a past life regressionist and was inundated with people wishing to know "what they had been" in a past life. I would generally try to explain that a past life regression was not always a pleasant experience. In fact, I had discovered that a necessary sadness usually accompanied each occurrence. Through experience, I eventually came up with a pattern of events that seemed to take place in the individual's life prior to each regression episode. And, if the regression was permitted to take its course, the individual recognized the unresolved issues (karma) and, finally, acknowledged them.

I have found that, prior to each experience, one of our guides tends to draw closer to us. They may even be the soul who shared the lifetime with us in which the lesson was not completed and is now being brought to the surface. They are there to help us work out the unresolved karma, and while doing so, provide us comfort while going through the process. While working with the person, I utilize this guide to help answer questions and to show me the issue that needs to be settled. Keep in mind that I am only a bystander in this process. The real issue lies within the person them self, and must be recognized by the individual as something that needs to be brought back to the surface so that the lesson which was unfinished in the past can now be completed.

The following is an account of the "strange incident" described in Section 1 (You Have Got to Believe)

THE DOCTOR IS IN

On one of my visits to a psychic, I was told there was a Joseph who watched over me. Since I had not really grasped the concept of spirit guides at the time, and I did not have any relative who had died by the name Joseph, I just brushed it off as an error on her part. It was not until years later that I would realize just how wrong I had been.

I had come into this life with the aspiration to be a "baby" doctor and that, as a child, is exactly how I would describe it to anyone who would ask. As I got older, I started to use the term Pediatrician, which I would later find out to be a misnomer.

As mentioned earlier in the book, while attending a class on spirit guides in the early 1980's, there had been one lesson that described how our guides might try to come in contact with us. As noted, the instructor explained that if we were not responding to the usual "signs", we might just wind up with a headache as a result of their "pounding" upon our heads to get our attention. Prior to attending this course I had set up an appointment to do some volunteer work in a hospital, which was scheduled for the weekend following this particular class. I showed up early for my appointment very eager to embark on my anticipated career path. Upon my arrival I found that I was to be assigned to the OB/GYN Unit. When I got to the unit, I was advised that there was a delivery taking place, and I stood eagerly waiting for the birth and the chance to actually see a new born baby. I heard the cry from the other side of the delivery room door and stood frozen in my spot as they brought the baby through. My first glimpse was of a small screaming child covered in what seemed to be some sort of mucus. As I got closer, I chanced to glance over at the freshly cut umbilical cord…at which point I passed out cold on the floor.

Now allow me to backtrack a bit and tell you a little about myself. I am a person who is far from squeamish. I have pulled pieces of metal out of my own leg, and watched as others have ripped holes in their arms, legs, and heads. I have even replaced a piece of my own finger after slicing it open with a razor blade, and this all before the tender age of 14; so for me to pass out at the age of 21 at the sight of a simple umbilical cord was a blow to my ego. I left the hospital that day, once they scraped me off the floor, in a complete state of depression. My whole life's ambition had been taken away from me with the cry of a child. What was I to do now? It was in this disheartened state of mind that I returned to class the next week; and it was during this class that I had my first "past life regression" experience.

At the point in the story detailed in Section 1 where Jan advised me of my "visitor", the same point where the room around me seemed to disappear, I found myself "watching" a scene of a young girl standing on a porch calling out to someone across a field. The sky was dark and lightning flashed everywhere as the rain poured from above. As I looked out into the field, I saw what appeared to be a man dressed in a dark over coat and a hat pulled down over his face to shelter him from the rain. As he came closer I noticed that he was carrying a bag, a doctor's bag. As he ran across the field the young girl screamed out to him to hurry. I then flashed over to the scene taking place inside of the house. What I saw there was a woman in the last stages of childbirth having a difficult time delivering the baby. The young terrified girl was her only companion and, as they say in the movie, "didn't know nothin' about birthin no babies." Therefore, their only hope was this young doctor charging toward the house; but, unfortunately, he was never to reach his patient. You see, with the strike of one quick flash of lightning, he fell dead to the ground.

I watched in horror as the young girl screamed out into the cold harsh night, and turned back towards the house as she realized that she did not scream alone. It was at this point that the women made her last push; a push that would result in the death of both mother and child.

The young girl fell to the floor covered in blood, staring at the motionless child in her arms; staring down at the umbilical cord still attached to the mother. A sensation of recognition came over me and suddenly the realization hit; the young girl in the scene was me in a different lifetime. It was at this point that I understood my reason for wanting to be a "baby doctor" in this lifetime, so that I would never find myself in that situation again. It was also at this point that I had found my Joseph (the doctor), who, because of his inability to help me then, had decided to stick around and watch over me through this lifetime; and I remember to thank him everyday for that decision.

ARIANA'S JOURNEY BACK

A friend of mine, whom I will call Ariana, had come to be extremely interested in the subject of parapsychology. We would sit for hours and discuss topics such as meditation, spiritual guides, and karma. One area in which Ariana was having difficulty in her personal life was the issue surrounding relationships. She was in her late twenties and had yet to develop anything that was worth discussing. I did notice, however, that she would spend days upon days reading romance novels. Each time I would ask her about her own ideal of "Mr. Right" she would always have the same description—dark hair and green eyes.

On her first visit to my home, while we were meditating, Ariana experienced a pain in her left shoulder area, which I was also experiencing. The sensation did not make sense at the time, but, ultimately, the explanation would come. Almost two years later Ariana came to me and told me about a dream she had. It seemed more than an ordinary dream so we decided that during the next week each evening Ariana should come to me and tell me about her dreams. Each dream seemed to be a piece of a puzzle, which we would find would eventually fit together. One afternoon after work, as Ariana sat in my office discussing her latest dream, I noticed a presence sitting in the chair next to her. When I told her about him, Ariana asked me to find out what they wanted. The presence advised me that he was Ariana's guide, and that they had come to help her resolve her past life issue. Needless to say, Ariana was doubtful. She asked me to have this guide, whom we will call Michael, answer a question that she had brought up the prior evening during a meditation (in other words the very much sought after VALIDATION). Michael became annoyed that Ariana was employing me as a "go-between" instead of utilizing her own abilities to speak with him, but finally gave her the answer she sought.

As the week progressed Ariana and I kept in close touch, and we decided that the reason for these dreams needed further investigation. The subject of past life regression had come up several times in our conversations, and we came to the conclusion that maybe this was a point in time where it would be useful. Within the next month we found the perfect opportunity to begin our exploration.

I would like to pause for a moment in the story to caution the reader and remind you to make sure that there is a protection meditation done prior to the regression and a cleansing meditation done after.

The meditation began with me handing Ariana a box of tissues, which I informed her she might need during the course of the evening. I also had several other people in the room who I asked to "keep watch" over the proceedings. At one point in the meditation I began to see what Ariana was seeing. I remained a bystander to make sure she was all right. At one point I saw her back off and pull out of the meditation. Not wanting to alarm the others, I proceeded to go around the room, as I usually do after any meditation session, and question each person on what they had experienced. When I reached Ariana, she seemed to leave out a very important part of her meditation, the part that I had also observed. When I questioned her she hesitated, and said that she did not want to confront what she had seen. I told her that these details were a very important part of the regression process, and that if she wanted to resolve the issues, she must continue. I assured her that I would be with her each step of the way.

The meditation progressed, and many questions were answered. Unfortunately, like a bad ending to a movie, I must end the story here, for each individual is ensured his or her right to privacy. Needless to say, Ariana discovered the reason behind the pain she had originally experienced in her arm, her dreams, and most important, her relationship issues. I can tell you though that she now finds herself in a very fulfilling relationship with a very different "Mr. Right."

PART II

When all is complete and fairly done

Inspiration comes in to enlighten one

Inspiration, where does it draw from? Who controls that little voice inside one's head and leads them on the path of creativity? Is it drawn from the subconscious mind of the individual, or could it be possible that there is some "muse" from another dimension assisting them down the path? Could this actually be possible? Even Webster's Dictionary gives reference to this ideal with its definition of the word inspire which reads in part, "…to cause, guide, communicate, or motivate as by divine or supernatural influence." For over twenty years I have followed these ideals and have been working on improving on my communication skills with these guides of the unseen realm through meditation.

One Friday evening in October in 1995 I received what seemed to be a children's story during one such meditation. I wrote this story down in a journal which was given to me by a close friend and mentor. When the meditation ended I read the story out loud to the meditation group. As it turned out, what seemed to me to be a simple story held a different meaning for each individual in the room, and in some way answered a concern for something that had currently been going on in his or her life. After some contemplation, I decided that these stories were messages from another realm and that they should be shared with anyone who might be comforted by them in some way.

Therefore, I have chosen to dedicate the second part of this book to sharing these stories with the reader so that, maybe, they too will gain some solace or inspiration from their retelling.

THE PROMISE OF A
FUTURE

Once there was a little girl who ran through a valley and came to a cliff. When she looked out over the cliff there was a dry, unfertile desert for as far as she could see. But as the little girl stood and watched, a pine tree popped up…first one, then another, and another, until the once barren land turned into a beautiful forest. And the little girl was happy. However, as she stood there fascinated by the splendor of the view, man came and cut down all the trees until once again the land was barren. And the little girl was sad.

But as the little girl watched, a flower grew up from the once again arid soil,…first one, then another,…and another…, until the land before the little girl blazed into a vision of multi-colored brilliance. And the little girl was happy. But suddenly a group of children came along and picked all the flowers, again leaving the land a vast void of nothingness. And once again the little girl was sad.

But as the little girl watched in sorrow, a drop of rain fell…first one, then another, and another, until the void was filled leaving a beautiful ocean, with seagulls flying overhead, and fish flourishing within. And once again, the little girl smiled. But along came man, who polluted the waters and depleted the ozone, causing all the water to dry up, leaving all the fish to die. And once more the little girl was sad.

Suddenly, as the little girl stood drying her tears, she looked out into the once again dry desert, and saw a tiny animal crawl up out of a hole, first one, then another….

So remember little girl, the earth was meant to live, and no matter how many times it is brought down to depletion, it will survive to bring life to another day. THERE'S ALWAYS THE PROMISE OF A FUTURE.

THE STORY OF GREY RABBIT

Once there was a little grey rabbit that was always fearful of the dangers that lurked outside his door. Therefore, he decided early in life that he would stay tucked comfortably inside his burrow and only venture outside when it was absolutely necessary. When these times arose he would scurry out, get what he needed, and return as soon as possible. He never stopped to make friends, or bothered to look around and notice the beauty of the world around him.

One winter morning, on one such endeavor, Grey Rabbit happened to run into a little brown rabbit, who smiled cheerfully at him. However, fearing that something dreadful would befall him, Grey Rabbit just brushed passed him slamming his door behind him. But when he was tucked safely inside, Grey Rabbit peered outside his window just in time to see Brown Rabbit frolicking with his young brothers and sisters. Suddenly, a giant hawk swooped down and grabbed one of the bunnies. Grey Rabbit watched in terror and sadness as the rabbits outside wept for their lost sibling. "See I knew there was danger outside," Grey Rabbit sighed to himself, "just imagine, that could have been me!" And with that, Grey Rabbit's ventures outside became even more infrequent.

One beautiful spring afternoon, as Grey Rabbit sat reading a book, he happened to glance outside and saw Brown Rabbit playing with his friends. They seemed to be having so much fun that for a moment Grey Rabbit felt a twinge of loneliness. But just as he began to rise out of his chair and walk toward the door, the memory of that winter morning flashed before his eyes and he scrambled to slam the door shut. "No, I must stay inside, for the outdoors only holds danger, and in my home I will be safe," he explained to himself.

As the years went by, quite often Grey Rabbit would find himself sitting at the window watching as Brown Rabbit made new friends, fell in love, became a father, and eventually grow old.

One day, many years later, as Grey Rabbit struggled out of his chair for a warm glass of milk, he noticed Brown Rabbit laboring along the path outside his window with his grandchildren. He smiled, for even though they had never spoken a word to each other, in some way he felt connected to Brown Rabbit. In a strange way Brown Rabbit was the only friend he had ever had. Suddenly, a shot rang out hitting Brown Rabbit and killing him instantly in his tracks. A heavy despair fell over Grey Rabbit and he toiled off sadly to bed. That night Grey Rabbit died in his sleep.

After you have finished this story I ask that you sit back and contemplate the following question... Which of the two rabbits had a happier life?

A FLIGHT TO HEAVEN

Once there was a little caterpillar named George who would sit in the trees and watch the birds soar high above in the beautiful blue sky. One day while he sat gazing at the heavens, a splendid white dove landed on a nearby branch with some twigs in its beak. As George watched, the dove began to build a nest. "Could I be of some assistance?" George asked. "Sure," said the dove, "I'm having some difficulty keeping the twigs together." "Oh I have just the solution," George responded, and with that he began to spin his sticky strands binding the twigs together in a tight hold. "Gee, thank you," exclaimed the dove, noticing the wonderful job George had done. "Ah, it was nothing," George answered shyly. "Can I ask you something?" questioned George. "What is it like flying up in the clear blue sky, being lighter than air?" "Oh, it is wonderful!" the dove stated excitedly. "Especially when I fly into Heaven and visit with God." "You've seen God?" George asked in amazement. "Oh yes," answered the dove, "I have stood in His light. Heaven is a glorious place." "Wow!" thought George. Just then he noticed a group of ants struggling to get something in their ant hole. "Hold on, I will be right back," George told the dove. "I want to see if I can lend them a hand." After taking a moment to think, George slid from the tree branch to the floor and began to run toward the anthill. "Look out!" he cried, and with the aid of his numerous legs, George built up enough speed to shove the food into the hole. "Gee thanks George," shouted the lead ant. "No trouble," George called out as he headed back to the dove. "That was very kind of you to help," the dove stated when George reached the branch. "Ah, it was nothing," answered George in his usual nonchalant manner. "But getting back to flying, is it really as awesome as it looks?" "Oh yes," said the dove, "maybe someday you will know the feeling." "Probably not," George said sadly, "but it's all right, I can always dream." "I have to leave you now," he said coming out of his melancholy thoughts. "I promised to bring some food over to a sick old beetle, but it has been great talking to you." "You are very kindhearted, George," answered the dove. "Ah, it's nothing," waved George with a flick of his wrist. "Bye George," called back the dove.

Years later the dove returned to the tree looking for George but found no one. Suddenly a beautiful butterfly fluttered down into his path. "Hey dove, how have you been?" asked the butterfly. "George, is that you?" recognizing the voice. "Yeah, it's me. Look what happened, I got wings!" "So I've noticed," said the dove. "You know the first thing I did?" said George. "I flew straight to heaven, and you know who I saw?" "No, who George?" asked the dove. "I saw God!" George said proudly. "That is great, George," said the dove with a smile. "What did He say to you?" questioned the dove. "Well, it was sort of strange," said George. "He didn't say anything, He just smiled at me. Why do you think that was? Do you think He didn't recognize me?" "Oh, I'm sure He knew who you were, George," responded the dove. "But don't worry about it George, just enjoy your wings!" With that George fluttered happily away. As he did, the dove whispered after him, "No, George, all your kindness wasn't nothing, *it was something!*"

THE HEALING POT

In the middle of a forest there sat a little village. On the outskirts of this village lived an old woman whom many believed to be crazy. Each day the woman would walk briskly through the town carrying a small black empty pot yelling, "Heal thyself. Know the secrets and heal thyself."

It happened that a small child from the village became very ill and everyone in the town, including the doctors, had all but given up on her chances for survival. One day, while running to the market, the mother of the child found herself standing face to face with the old woman. "Do you wish to know the secret of healing?" asked the old woman. "I will teach you if you will allow me." At this point the mother had become so desperate that she was willing to try anything. "Would you come to my home this evening and see my child?" she begged. "Certainly," responded the old woman. "Expect me when the clock strikes eight." And with those words the old woman turned and walked away.

That evening at precisely eight o'clock a knock came at the door. When the mother opened the door and her husband saw who it was, he began to speak out and tell the crazy old woman to go beg somewhere else. "Please John, do not say a word," his wife quietly pleaded. "I asked her to come." With that the husband just stood there mumbling something about crazy women.

The old woman breezed in through the door carrying her old black cauldron. As she passed by the couple, they peeked into the pot and saw that it was empty as always. "Where is the child?" the old woman questioned. The mother led her to her daughter's small bedroom. When they reached the room they found the pale child lying in the bed taking short shallow breaths. The old woman quickly went to work, rolling up her sleeves, and taking a clean white rag from her old coat pocket. She dipped the rag into the empty cauldron and brought it out twisting it into a knot as if she were wringing a liquid out of it. "What is she doing?" whispered John. "She is crazy. Why have you brought this lunatic into our home?" he cried. "Be quiet!" whispered the mother anxiously. As she watched, the old woman carefully placed the rag upon the child's head reciting a little prayer. When she finally finished, she turned to the couple and said, "You must do exactly as I have done for the next twelve hours. On the stroke of each hour dip the cloth into the pot, wring it out and place it on the child's head once more," she instructed. "I shall return in the morning." With that she walked briskly out the door closing it behind her. The couple stared after her, then turned to look at their child. The mother glanced at her husband with a pleading look in her eyes and they both went to work imitating each of the old woman's actions. All through the night, at the stroke of the new hour, the parents toiled going through the motions as the old woman had instructed, and never forgetting to complete the task with a little prayer. After the completion of the twelfth hour each fell asleep at the foot of their daughter's bed.

Suddenly they found themselves being shaken awake from their exhausted slumber. As they opened their eyes trying to focus on the commotion, they discovered themselves staring in amazement at the sight of their child bouncing happily upon her bed. "It's a miracle!" cried John with tears in his eyes. With that a loud knock came at the door, and in strolled the old woman. "I don't know how to thank you," the mother said to the old woman. "Just look at our child, you have performed a miracle!" The old woman just grinned back at her and walked over to collect her rag and her empty pot. Before turning to leave, she smiled down into the eyes of the once ill child and then left the house without a word.

When news of the miraculous healing reached the town, the old woman was called upon time and time again to assist in the healing of the sick. Each time the same thing would happen. She would arrive in the evening at precisely eight o'clock with her empty pot and a clean white rag. She would give her instructions before leaving and then come back in the morning. In each instance she would return to find the patient healed, collect her belongings, and leave without a word.

Years later the mother of the sick child came upon the old woman once again at the market. With determination she walked over to question the old woman about something that had been bothering her over those many years. "Forgive me," she said. "From that very first night I have wondered, and I find that I must finally ask, what it is that you put into that black cauldron that heals so many people in so many different ways?" "Oh, many things," exclaimed the old woman. "But it is not what I put in that does the healing," she explained. "It is what you, and many others, have put in that gets the job done." The mother looked at the woman in confusion and said, "What I put in? But I put nothing in, we only did as you instructed." "Oh, but you are wrong. You all put in the most important ingredient," responded the old woman. "I do not understand," declared the mother. "What ingredient are you talking about?" The old woman just smiled back at her and turned to leave, but before she did she simply stated, "You put in your faith." And with that she walked off into the crowd.

HEAVEN'S SMILE

This story opens on a clown who traveled throughout the world with a famous circus. Each night the clown would put on his makeup and costume and go out into the arena giving all he could to make the audience laugh. However, as he pranced around with the other clowns, all he would see were several people leaving for refreshments and busily chatting to each other. He would sometimes have the feeling that he was only there to fill up space until the next act came along. Each evening as he sat in his dressing room wiping away the makeup, he would ask himself questions. "Why don't they notice me? What am I doing wrong? Maybe I just wasn't cut out to be a clown!" Needless to say, most nights the clown would go home depressed.

However, on one particular night as he again sat questioning himself in the mirror on his worth in the circus life, he noticed a mother with her small child standing behind him. As he turned to them the mother asked "How can someone who brings such joy to others be so sad?" "What are you talking about?" asked the clown "Nobody ever really pays attention to me, I just fill up the empty space." "How can you say this?" the mother responded in amazement. "Just look at the smile on my child's face; it wasn't there when we came in tonight. Don't you know that when you make a child smile, the angels in Heaven smile too?" "I never knew that," answered the clown thoughtfully. "Well now you do," the mother stated simply. "So from now on, instead of seeing those who don't see you, look to the children; they will help ease your sense of doubt." With that the mother took her child's hand, but before leaving, the child turned back and gave the clown the most angelic smile he had ever seen.

From that night on, each time the clown performed, he would seek out the children in the audience. Each time he spotted one he would lose all his self-doubt and know true happiness. As he scanned the arena he would see thousands of smiles emanating from the children's faces. Seeing each one he would know that the angels in Heaven, and God, would be smiling too. What better audience could he possibly ask for?

A LITTLE BIT OF
KNOWLEDGE

Once upon a time a little fish was on an outing with his mother, father, sisters and brothers. During their venture something shiny and sparkly caught his eye, so he wandered off to follow it. Up, up, up he went after the glittering prize. As he neared the surface and was close enough to touch it, Little Fish reached out with his fin and without warning found himself caught on a fisherman's hook. Something began to pull at him and the harder he struggled, the more entangled he became. Out of the water he was drawn, flipping and floundering all around. "Please, oh please, someone help me," he cried. "I do not want to die!" Then with a spontaneous burst of energy, Little Fish broke free and quickly swam back to the safety of the bottom of the sea, complaining and swearing to all those around him that he would never venture up to the surface again.

A few years later, while out with his friends, Little Fish noticed that the waters up above were unusually dark and in the distance he could hear a faint rumble. Forgetting about his vow of the past, up, up, up he swam. All at once, the waters began to churn and Little Fish found himself surrounded by terrible noise and flashing lights while being tossed and turned. "Oh, how did I get myself into this danger?" he cried. "If I get out safely, I will never return again," he promised himself. Suddenly the sea began to calm, and Little Fish swam down to the quiet safety of the waters below.

In another instance, as before, Little Fish's attention was caught by something above. Up, up, up he swam, only to find himself covered in the foulest smelling slime he had ever encountered. Struggling to swim and breathe, he became extremely annoyed. Without realizing why, he began to spin quickly and the slime started to fall away. When he became free, he dove down into the dark waters and the protection of home, once again complaining and vowing never to return.

As time passed, however, Little Fish would for some reason or another, forget his promise and find himself drawn back to the surface. Each occurrence would find him, again, in some dangerous predicament, only to be saved from harm at the last moment. And, as with each time before, he would return to the safety of the waters below vowing to never return again.

One day, long into his older years, one of Little Fish's friends heard him complaining to another about all the experiences he had encountered near the surface. "If it is so terrible, why do you keep returning?" asked his friend. "Because through the years," explained Little Fish, "I find that, even though I have faced these dilemmas, which usually result in fear and anxiety, I have been able to free myself and return to the safety of home. I also have found that each time, upon returning to my shelter, I have brought back with me a little bit of knowledge." "But is it really worth all the trouble?" the friend queried. "And if so, why do you always complain about it?" "It certainly is!" exclaimed Little Fish. "For with that bit of knowledge comes an energy and strength which helps me go through the next phase of my life." "Then why complain?" returned the friend. Little Fish just smiled back and said, "That reminds me of just how alive I am!"

BLANKET OF THE SOUL

This is a story about a little girl named Sally who was given a very special gift. Sally's first memory was when she was five years old. She fell and cut herself very badly and had to be rushed to a hospital. When she got home her mother cradled her in her arms and rocked her to sleep. When Sally awoke in the morning she found a beautifully colored ball of yarn at the bottom of her bed. She grabbed the string and put it away in her special box of trinkets.

When Sally was twelve years old she developed her first crush. She told all her friends and for months she followed this little boy around, only to one day be told by a friend that he had asked another girl in school out on a date. Sally ran home with tears streaming down her face, threw herself on her bed and cried herself to sleep. When she awoke in the morning she found another ball of colored string at the bottom of her bed, and again she tucked it away in her special box.

As time went on Sally grew into a woman. She fell in love; this time for real, got married, and had children of her own. And just as before, each time a crisis arose that would lead to heartache for Sally, she would wake up the following morning to discover another ball of splendidly colored yarn on her bed. However, as she grew older, and the pain deeper, the ball of yarn would be larger. One day while rummaging through her special box, which now had grown in size because of the numerous balls of yarn, Sally got an idea and scurried off to find her crocheting needle.

Years later, as Sally lay on her deathbed surrounded by her children and their families, she called out for her five-year-old great-granddaughter, Mary. She bent over and whispered something into the child's ear, and the small child scrambled from the bed and over to a chest positioned at the bottom of Sally's bed. To the amazement of the others in the room, Mary pulled out the most beautiful blanket they had ever seen, and brought it to Sally in her bed. Sally took the blanket, nestled down in the bed, and covered herself with it. When Sally's oldest child questioned her mother where the blanket had come from, in her last breath, Sally responded, *"It is the blanket of my soul."* With that Sally slipped away with a smile on her lips, drifting slowly into the light.

THE GIFT

Once there was a little girl named Mary. Throughout her life Mary had spent most of her time with her Nana. During those years, as Mary grew, her Nana would always be walking by her side, laughing, singing, chatting or just quietly holding Mary's hand. For almost all of her life, Mary had been happy and enjoyed living.

But the day came when Mary's Nana was gone. No longer would they spend long days on a beach or telling stories late into the night. Mary became very sad and, eventually, her sadness turned to anger. Anger toward others who still had happiness, anger at herself, but most of all, anger at God. "Why is He such a cruel God that he took away my Nana when I was not ready to give her up?" she would wonder.

Eventually Mary began to turn all others away. She became reclusive and would not allow herself to feel love toward another. "Why bother?" she would ask, "I will only lose them too!"

One fall day Mary sat alone on a park bench deep in the woods. She watched as the leaves fell from the trees, withered and dry, to the ground. When she looked up she noticed a stranger staring down at her. Mary noticed that there was something odd about him; it was as if his face were surrounded with a mysterious glow. "Why do you sit alone in such darkness?" the stranger asked. "Just go away and leave me alone!" Mary snapped back. "What has brought you such sadness and anger, my child?" the stranger questioned. "Why do you seek out solitude and loneliness? You are too young to be so closed down and alone." "What else should I be?" Mary responded. "Evidently God wants us to exist like this! Why else would he make us know love, and then take it away?" "Take it away?" the stranger asked. "Have you never seen or felt the gift He has given to us?" "What gift?" Mary sneered back. "Close your eyes Mary," the stranger instructed. Not knowing why, and wondering at the same time how he knew her name, Mary complied with his request. "Now stand up and take my hand, but before you do, take this box in your other hand. But do not open the box until I tell you to." With that Mary felt herself being lead down one flight of steps, then another, and finally one more. "Where did these steps come from?" Mary whispered to herself. "Open your eyes Mary," the stranger said. As she did, Mary found herself staring at an old wooden door. "Open the door Mary," the stranger instructed. Mary began to tug at the door, and at first found that it would not budge. However, after several tries, it began to open. "Now go inside," she heard the voice say. "But it is dark and cold in there!" Mary snapped back. "Then take this lantern," he said. Mary held up the light into the darkened room, only to discover that it was empty. "Where have you brought me?" Mary screamed. "It is alright Mary, go to the table and open the box," the voice instructed. "What table…" she started to scream back, but as she did, a table appeared in the middle of the room. Mary went to the table and began to open the box. As she did the room filled with a warm, soft light. "Hello Mary dear," she heard a familiar voice say. "Nana?" Mary whispered. As she looked up she saw her grandmother standing in the corner of the room. Mary ran to her and hugged her as she had never hugged another in a very long time. "I have missed you so much," Mary said with tears spilling down her face. "What do you mean, Mary?" her grandmother responded. "I have been here waiting for you." "HERE! Where are we?" Mary questioned. "In your heart, Mary," she heard the stranger respond. "In my heart?" "Yes, Mary. You see God gives us a wonderful gift at birth; that gift is our memories. They start from the moment we are born, and follow us through life until we are gone. We store them within our hearts, and whenever we need their help to remember something or someone very dear to us, all we need do is close our eyes and visit our heart. They will always be there, and nothing can ever take them away from us."

Mary found such happiness and solace within the stranger's words that she put her head down into her hands and cried. However, instead of being tears of sadness, which they had been for such a long time, these tears were tears of joy. When she did eventually lift her head and open her eyes, Mary found that she was once again back on the bench in the woods, except now something was different. She realized that she now felt as if the weight of the world had been lifted from her shoulders. "Remember Mary," she heard her Nana's voice say. Mary smiled and said, "Oh, don't worry Nana, I'll be back." With that, Mary got up from the bench and walked cheerfully down the path, noticing for the first time the beautiful colors of those leaves still left on the trees.

LIGHT OF HOPE

There once was an old vagrant who traveled from town to town carrying an old unlit lantern. As he journeyed through each town he would randomly stop at a home and knock. "Good day, will you help out an old man and be kind enough to light my lamp?" he would inquire. And each time, upon observing the bedraggled old man, the response would be the same. "Go away you crazy old fool!" would be yelled to him as the door slammed in his faced.

One cold night, however, he ventured upon a small house in need of much repair. He walked up the weed-covered path and knocked on the door. A young woman opened the door and asked, "May I help you?" "Will you light my lamp?" responded the old man. "Oh, I do not know if I can, but come inside out of the cold and let me see if we can find a way," replied the woman. As the two entered, a small child burst into the room. "Mama, please come finish the story with me!" cried the child as he danced under her feet. "Just a moment," answered the woman, "I have to see if I can help this gentleman with his lamp first." "O.K." the child said looking at the man with a smile, and with that he ran back into his bedroom. "Are you alone here?" questioned the vagrant. "Yes, my husband died a few years back," the woman stated with a sad look in her eyes. "How do you get by all alone with a young child?" asked the man. "Oh, I manage all right," she exclaimed, "I fill my home with love, face each day with faith that we will be provided for, and, with a little hard work, I find that each morning brings us a new day." At this point the woman looked closely at the old vagabond and gently prodded "But, enough about me, when was the last time you had something to eat, or slept in a warm bed? Come sit by my fire and warm your cold bones and I will get you something to eat. It may not be much, but I'm sure I can find a little something."

A short time later, after he had warmed himself and filled his stomach, the man stood up, thanked the woman for her courtesy and headed towards the door. "Wait," the woman called after him, "What about your lamp? Did you not ask if I could help you light it?" And to her surprise, as the man turned and faced her, she saw that the lantern was shining with the brightest light she had ever seen. "How can that be?" she asked in disbelief. "How can that be?" he repeated, "I'm surprised that you of all people should ask me that question!" he responded with a smile. "All it needed was a little HOPE!" With that, he opened the door and walked out into the cold night illuminating the darkness with his awe-inspiring lantern.

TAKE TIME TO NOTICE

Once upon a time there was a little boy named Chao. Each day Chao's mother would take him to a beautiful field where she would gather herbs for her home. And each day Chao would pass the time by sulking and grumbling about having to waste his time picking flowers instead of playing at home with his friends. One day, while in the field, Chao came upon a wondrous garden, but instead of seeing the beauty around him, he just slumped down on the ground chopping the flowers around him. Just then he noticed an old man sitting on a stone bench across from him. "Why do you grumble and fret so young man?" asked the elder. "My mom makes me come here everyday instead of letting me play back home with my friends. It's such a waste of time!" complained Chao. "Oh, I see," responded the old man. "Is this such a terrible place to be?" he continued. "There is nothing to do here. It is so boring!" snapped back Chao. "How about me telling you a story?" asked the old man. "Sure, I've got nothing better to do," grumbled Chao.

"Once there were two friends, a seagull and a fish," began the old man. "Each day the seagull would swoop down on a rock and visit with his friend. This one particular day found the fish in a solemn mood. "What is the matter my friend?" asked the seagull. "Oh, I don't know," answered the fish. "Sometimes I wonder why I am forced to spend my life swimming around in the ocean." "What? Are you kidding?" exclaimed the seagull. "I would love to be able to swim along the bottom of the ocean floor and see all the treasures it has to offer!" "Well, I have never really thought about it that way," said the fish thoughtfully. "But what about you? You can fly through the heavens and feel the warm sun on your wings," the fish continued. "You know what?" responded the seagull staring at the sunset. "I never

really took the time to notice." "Well, I guess it's time to go back down," *said the fish excitedly. "Yeah, I'll see you tomorrow," called back the seagull* *taking off towards the clouds. And on that day each one learned that* *instead of dwelling on the limitations of their surroundings, they should* *take the time to notice the rewards their worlds had to offer," finished the* *old man.*

"Hey, that was a great story!" exclaimed Chao. "Thanks for telling it, but I have to be off now, my mom is probably looking for me." With that Chao stood up and ran off toward the field. Suddenly he turned back to the old man and asked, "Are you going to be here tomorrow?" "Probably," replied the old man. "O.K., I'll see you then," said Chao. "Goodbye," said the old man with a grin. As he watched Chao head off, he overheard the boy say to himself, "Wow, I never noticed there were so many caterpillars around here! I'll have to remember to catch myself some tomorrow."

FOOTPATH OF COLOR

When my time had come and I ventured into the light, I was taken by an angel to a long footpath down which I could not see very far ahead. When I questioned the angel, he just pointed and gestured as if I should walk on.

After walking for what seemed a brief period of time, I found myself surrounded in the loveliest shade of blue. "I remember this color," I said to myself, "It was the color of my first party dress, when I was a young child." As I walked a little further I found myself encompassed in sunshine yellow. "Oh, I remember this color," I smiled, "This was the color of the roses in my prom corsage." The memories gave me a warm happy feeling inside, and I ventured on.

Further down the pathway a brilliant white light enveloped me. Once again I was washed over in happy memories. "This was the color of my beautiful wedding dress, and those wonderful winter mornings." I was so delighted with the splendid feelings I was experiencing, I suddenly found myself skipping.

But my pace slowed as I found myself venturing into a simple shade of grey. I could not really express my feelings at this hue of color; I just remember experiencing a familiar feeling of uncertainty and doubt. "Where was I going? Was I happy with my life? Why must we endure suffering in life?" With persistence I hurried ahead, not enjoying these memories as before.

I then found myself encircled by the most magnificent shade of pink. "Oh, this is a wonderful color," I exclaimed, "This is the color I knew when my first child was born." And once again, I was content.

As I proceeded on I began to feel that my journey was almost complete. Suddenly, I stopped dead in my tracks. "Oh no, not this color, don't make me remember this color! This reminds me of that terrible time, please God," I cried, "I have gone through it once; please do not make me experience it again." I began to run....

When I finally looked up, I found myself running on a beach. With tears streaming down my face, I began to slow down. "Why God, why did you make me remember?" I cried. Just then the angel returned to my side. He wrapped me in his arms and gestured toward the sky. As I looked up I saw the most exquisite rainbow I had ever seen. *"Never forget that it takes an assortment of colors to make a rainbow,"* the angel explained, *"Just as it takes an assortment of memories to make a life."*

MELODY FROM WITHIN

There once was a great concert pianist who was very famous for his talent. However, no matter how well he played, even though the audience adored him, he was never totally satisfied with his performance. As he took his bows, he was always walked off stage with a feeling of emptiness within his heart.

One winter evening, after one of his performances, he decided that instead of his usual limousine ride, he would walk home in the snow. As he turned down an alley he heard the most splendid melody he had ever heard. As he searched for the source of this divine sound he came upon a small house. He walked up to the house and peered through the window. There he saw a young child seated on a bench playing a piano. He tapped on the window to get the child's attention so that he might inquire as to the title of this beautiful song; however, the child just continued to play. He then walked to the doorway and knocked, but again he was ignored. After becoming impatient at what he felt was rudeness on the child's part, he opened the door and called out for attention; but still the child played on. Just as he was about to march in and reprimand the child on his persistent disrespect, an old woman walked into the room. Seeing the well-dressed man standing red faced in her living room, she ran over to him to see what he wanted. "I have been trying to get this child's attention for some time now to inquire what melody he was playing but as you can see he is totally ignoring me. Has no one taught him any manners?" the man demanded. "You see I have been a pianist most of my life, and a very well known authority in the field of music; however, I have never heard this exquisite tune. How can such a disrespectful child play such beautiful music?" "I beg your pardon sir, but this child is not being disrespectful, he is deaf and can not hear your questions," the woman explained. "What do you mean he is deaf? How can he play so beautifully without being able to hear? As I have informed you, I have been playing all my life, and I know you must be able to hear the music to understand it!" the man responded. "Ah, but are you happy with the sound you create?" the woman questioned simply. "When you play, you are playing with your hands and your ears. When this child plays, he uses his hands and his soul," the old woman continued, "And there is no music more beautiful than that which comes from within!" After taking a moment to fully understand what he had been told, the man turned slowly to leave. He took a moment to glance over at the piano and found that the child, who at this point had stopped playing, was smiling at him with the most wonderful smile he had ever seen.

From that day on the pianist trained himself to turn off his physical ears and draw his music from within his soul. Eventually he found that he not only played music that inspired others, but that he also played music that satisfied the emptiness within his heart.

A GOOD LESSON
LEARNED

One day a crow and a badger were wandering through the woods when they came upon a wolf with its leg caught in a trap. As they stood there the badger felt drawn to the wolf by the pain in his eyes and started to approach it. "What are your doing?" screeched the crow. "I am going to help him, can't you see how much pain he is in and how much he is suffering?" answered the badger. "So what, he's a wolf. If you help him out he will only return one day and kill you for his next meal," the crow responded. "How do you know that?" questioned the badger. He went further to explain, "I have heard that wolves are very loyal animals, and he may remember me and return the favor one day. You should learn that there are good and bad amongst our own kind too. Besides, the wolf kills for food or survival, not for fun. If you really think about it, isn't that what we all do in one way or another? Do you not kill the bug or the worm to eat or feed your young? Mr. Crow, you should really look into others and understand how they live. If you really try, you can see the reasons behind their actions and appreciate them for what they are."

"I don't care what you say, that loyalty bit is bogus, and that wolf is just a dumb animal that won't remember you the next time he sees you, especially if he is cold and hungry. All he will know is what a fool you are for trusting him and you'll be lunch!" the crow answered sarcastically. "You will see, he will eat you and your rose colored glasses!" With that the crow flew away.

The badger walked slowly over to the injured wolf and began to gnaw away at the leather straps of the trap. When it eventually snapped

85

open the wolf jumped up, knocking the badger over, and began to limp away. But before he had gotten fully out of sight, he turned back, looked the badger squarely in the eyes and stated simply, "I will remember," and then disappeared into the forest. The badger turned and walked off knowing that he had done what was right—what all beings, animal or man, should do. Learn for yourself about people, and do not be influenced by what others believe to be true.

DIFFERENT IS BETTER

Once there was a purple wildflower that grew in the middle of a beautiful garden of white roses along a well-traveled path. Each time a passerby came along, all the roses would stand tall and radiate their magnificent scent, which made the wildflower feel unattractive and insignificant. Day after day it was the same scenario, the roses would emanate beauty and the wildflower would grow more and more self-conscious; until eventually the wildflower realized that he would never be able to outshine the roses, so he began to slump over and wilt.

One day, as a garden fairy fluttered through the rose bed, she noticed the wilted wildflower and stopped to inquire, "Why do you slump over so wildflower?" "Look around me," answered the wildflower. "I am just something that grew by accident in the middle of these beautiful roses, a mistake. In fact, I should not be here at all, I only bring ugliness to the garden." "Oh, but that is not true, my friend," responded the fairy. "It is because of you that the garden is even more pleasing, for you are special. If there were only roses, what a dull garden this would be. Without your presence everyone who travels this path would only see white roses and, even though they are magnificent, it would tend to get uninteresting after a while." "I don't feel very special," mumbled the wildflower, "I only feel different." "You are different," answered the fairy. "However, do not feel that being different makes you less of a flower; know that your difference makes you exceptional. It is because of your difference that others are able to enjoy the diversity of God's universe, for without that diversity, what an unexciting place the world would be. You should stand tall and be proud of your unusual characteristics." "Oh, why bother," muttered the wildflower. "Nobody will ever notice me amongst these beautiful roses; they show the world what it truly means to be a flower." "You are so wrong," said the fairy. "It is amongst these roses that you will be noticed because you will catch their eye with your uniqueness." "Whatever you say," shrugged the wildflower with disbelief. "One day you will see what I mean," the fairy said with a smile. "Just hang in there," and with that the fairy fluttered away.

The very next day as the wildflower stood slumped over as usual, a young girl and her mother ventured along the path. "See the beautiful white roses, Annie?" said the woman. "Don't they smell superb?" "Yes, Mama, they smell pleasant," answered the child; but as she spoke she noticed the wildflower and ran over pointing to it with her small finger. "The roses are nice, but I like that pretty purple flower in the middle. All the roses are the same, but that flower is special. Can we take it with us?" The mother responded to the child's excitement with a smile on her face. "No, Annie. You are right, that flower is special; and because of that we should leave it here so that everyone else who travels this path can admire it too." "You're right, Mama. We should leave it here because it is so beautiful, but can we come by and see it again?" Seeing the eagerness on her child's face, the mother responded, "Certainly, Annie, and maybe we can bring some other friends to see it too." "I would like that, Mama," said the child as they both continued on down the path.

From that day on the wildflower stood tall and proud of his uniqueness, knowing in his heart that he was truly special; and that his being special made the world a better place to be.

I sat down, for I had a story to tell,

Now that it is finished, I hope I've done well.

But "The End" seems to be such an unhappy quote,

So I have chosen to close on a more positive note.

When reaching the page where words cease to be,

Sit down with a pen and some paper like me.

And share with the world your wisdom and thoughts,

Tell of the lessons you have thus far been taught.

But before you begin to tell your outlook,

Remember to pass on my little handbook.

Afterword

So there you have it, life (and afterlife) according to me. I hope that while reading this book you have laughed a little, and cried a little, because it is through emotions that we are able to "open up" and cleanse our souls.

Perhaps you read it because you are interested in understanding the beliefs of others, or because you are preparing an argument for a debate on the topic. Or maybe it just gave you the opportunity to pass the time while traveling or trying to fall asleep. Whatever the case, I hope that you found what you came for, and that you eventually find everything you seek out, including the peace of mind and body that we all pursue.

For those of you who are truly searching for answers, I hope that I have given you some suggestions on how you too might begin your spiritual journey on discovering just who you really are, and who might be traveling with you along the way.

Oh…one final thought. When you finally hear that message which comes as a "whisper in the night," remember to *pass it on*.

IN REMEMBRANCE

The day was warm under a clear blue sky,
They left their families with a kiss goodbye.
They entered a city overflowing with dwellers,
From the tops of skyscrapers to basement cellars.
They crossed the threshold of the mighty towers,
A symbol of freedom, an icon of power.
They began what seemed a normal day,
How were they to know the price they would pay?
At eight forty five their bodies were shaken,
As the engines roared, many lives were taken.
The confusion increased among them all
For those who were trapped, some made one last call.
They headed for stairs to descending floors.
They did not run, they had been here before.
Our bravest and finest came running in force,
To seek out some answers, to determine a source.
They pulled out the injured, the bleeding, the broken,
Or they just held a hand, no words need be spoken.
They looked to the towers as they heard the rumble,
Many stared in amazement as the skyline did tumble.
As they were consumed by the smoke and the ash,
They wondered at who would do something so rash.
What kind of person would perform such an act?
They must have no compassion, this was surely a fact.
As one day passed by and turned into another,
Many found they had lost a child, a brother.
But still they push on with faith and hope.
That some will be saved, it helps them to cope.
So we hold up our flags and wave them high,

We stand in the wreckage up to our thigh.
We gather donations to send to the crew,
We do everything that we can humanly do.
And we send out a message that is simple and plain.
They will always be with us, they have not died in vain.
And for those left behind to suffer the grief,
We will give them some comfort, we will send them relief.
And we'll shout to the world, to those who will hear it.
"You may shake our security, but you will not break our spirit!"

I live in an area of the Bronx where the view from my home takes in the Manhattan skyline in all its glory. The World Trade Center tragedy of September 11, 2001, took place while I was writing this book. Needless to say, this senseless act of terrorism affected our entire community, especially since this community includes many New York City firemen, police officers and other city workers. For weeks following the event I could not bring myself to even look out of my windows, and I fundamentally "closed down" my energy. Since I was having difficulty dealing with the "real pain" of those around me, I was not ready to deal with those who had passed over.

Eventually, a couple of individuals did come to me seeking answers and, contrary to my wishes, some energy did come through. I will not discuss any details, because, to put it simply, it is no one else's business but those involved. However, I can say this much…. they are ok…. and they want us to be too.

0-595-32501-7

Printed in the United States
102237LV00007B/248/A